Mother Language – Our Common Good

Initiative Contribution to SDGs Pschological Time and Space

Author; Tolofaina KudambangaMwanna

Declaration –

This is a social research in Mother Language – Our Common Good, a Project created not by a Scholar! There is a researcher/ Skills in Every Conscious Soul in Society given Development Background, but again, Skills is Lifelong Learning, every day we learn something new, knowingly or unknowingly. Consequently, never say never. Live to Learn. In this case, this Project is an ongoing process in the context of the unfolding initiative contribution to the SDGs Sustainable Development Goals.

All trademarks, design rights, copyrights, registered names, the logo, the symbols and the references sited remain property of their respective owners. This social research reserves the right to change the focus of this book; shut down; sell; and or change the terms of use at any time as deemed appropriate by the Brian-child; the Project-Team wholly reserves the right to update additional evidence if needed. This additional evidence may be in form of newly revealed historical facts, and or new observations, statistics etc. The research reserves the right to the inputs, delete and or changes required at any time deemed appropriate.

DEDICATION –

To the revered one.

Acknowledgement

Libation Pour to nTr – the Home and to whom Plenty Belongs

Libation Pour to our Spirit and Ancestors from whom we Learn.

Libation Pour for our daily struggles.

Libation Pour for the Youths Who Carry Our Promise for Tomorrow.

Nonetheless, with regards to them who Act otherwise.

To the revered one; Long live Son from Africa Soil; Kulwenzza-Otim. Long live Son in Africa Soil; Kulwenzza-Otim[1]. Long live son on Africa Soil; Kulwenzza-Otim. Long live rebirth of Africa Soil; Kulwenzza-Otim … to call A Name is to Invoke the Soul, for you are because we are moreover, we are because you are.

/Dd mdw in ink mAt Ra/

---

[1] Heroinic transposition of Nowell Christian-Merry Otim to Kulwenzza-Otim

Abbreviations

AVwDHA;	Added Value with Diaspora Home-Away
BCA;	Before Common Era
DSD;	Division for Sustainable Development Goals
EASG;	Education Academic Stakeholder Group
HLPF	High Level Political Forum
NGO;	None Government Organization
NAI;	Nordic Africa Institute
RBK21;	Re-Birth of Knowledge in the 21st century
SDG;	Sustainable Development Goals
UNESCO;	United Nations Educational, Scientific and Cultural Organization's International World Heritage program.

Transliteration from Ranykemet; Mother Language to English language

/ii.ti. m. Htp/	Welcome in peace.
/Htp di nsw.t/	Opening prayer/ Offering Formula/ Recitation in Ranykemet language at an opening of an event or ceremony. The length and or concept of the /Htp di nsw.t/ depends on the event.
/Dd mdw in ink mAt Ra/	Words spoken by I daughter of Ra/
/Km.t/	Black ↔ Coal ↔ Kemet ↔ Fertile Land etc.
/nTr/	Netcheru; God/ Life ↔ infinite ↔ existence, existence cannot exist yet deny the existence does not exist.
/mdw/	Words
/Ra/	using the Gardiner codes, we look in the Vygus dictionary and find N5 is /Ra = Sun or det. hrw, "day" or sw, "day" or N5 Det sun ↔ times ↔ Sun-god ↔ Enlightenment.
/sbA/	To teach, to instruct, to tend
/Saga/	Saga
/Shm.m. Htp/	Travel in peace.
/sSw/	Scribe ↔ write.
/sSw mdw nTr/	Scribe of Divine Words of Netcheru.

1).

Mother Language – Our Common Good

Initiative Contribution to SDGs for the "future we want" …

/ii. ti. m. Htp/ – Welcome in Peace

What is spoken language on Mother Knee, without regards to Mother Language – Our Common Good?

Many Africans are struggling with self-studies in Mother language in school corridors. This is both challenging and so on. Because details have it that the reason it is only in Africa where one finds Multilingual, could be Historical Africa is birthplace of Language. Think of the saying goes "a fruit will never fall far apart from the mother fruit tree itself, unless in one way or another this fruit was carried to destination." Arguably Spoken Languages become Monolingual(s), as one moves away from Africa.

Now that we are living the era of SDGs. Where SDG4 concerns quality education …

Now that we are living pschological era of the United Nations HLPF/ EASG June 2012 resolutions and outcome; "future we want" and back to SDG4 quality education – modern Africa will be disadvantaged if Africa is left to write down Africa Spoken Languages on Mother Knee disoriented from Mother Language; Ranykemet in Antiquity.

Something interesting in the World of development aid is that; Every Soul that becomes Conscious of Civilization soon want to go do development aid to Africa, with evidence – the, Missionaries, the Colonialism, current NGOs you name them, all want to go to do development aid to Africa. these civilized minds go to Africa for something in common amongst them which is disorient Africa Spoken Languages union with Mother Language in Antiquity. Swahili language was not introduced to Africa, rather Swahili Language was means to disorient Bantu languages from Mother Language in Antiquity. The ongoing

Western development aid of education to Africa is even more interesting – how development aid of education act as if they are ignorant of the fact that Indo-European languages are best studied with reference to a mother language in Antiquity. when this is the case, one is moved to see the bias of a development aid of education to Africa.

How about China?

Now, China knowing that the Great secret of Asia is revealed in the Book Title; "historical facts from Paekche's Principle – the Great Secret of Asia by Bayemy Biyick 2014"

China is on the go to do development aid in Africa but what is the difference between the western development aid goals to Africa or the China development aid goals to Africa given the unfolding historical facts from Paekche's Principle – the Great Secret of Asia by Bayemy Biyick 2014?

Then the questions become; are Africa States and Governments not to blame? Africa, if colonial languages are teachable in Africa why is it difficult to teach Ranykemet the Mother Language in Africa given the tools of SDG4 and "future we want"; resolution 183 concerning Africa?

Africa, what lesson did we learn from the MDG2015 United Nations pulled off Tools of implementation to solve the FGM phenomenon without a mention of why not introduce Africa Classic Studies so that the solutions to FGM are based on clear knowledge of Africa Worldview?

Objective

The Objective of 996234843-AVwDHA.Organization is; in the era of Mother Language UNESCO SDG4 quality education by 2030 is to affirm Africa states and governments, in their capacity and authority, to establish an inquiry in the United Nations; HLPF, EASG, NGOs etc. about the implementation of Mother Language UNESCO SDG4 quality education by 2030. This implementation must clearly concern (Africa) spoken languages reunion with Mother Language in Antiquity and a core priority in school curriculum. This is the imperative to put on an African Worldview in school core-curriculum, as a timely and clearly implemented SDG4 quality education by 2030, so that it becomes crystal clear in Africa and to the agents of development aid to Africa, that the strength and power of a people depend on the understanding from spoken language union with Mother Language. Take for example Indo-European languages care to teach their descendants how language does not just happen. Language was born from a mother in Antiquity.

Moreover, Africa must wise up to implement The United Nations June 2012 resolutions; "future we want" acknowledges; "... significant challenges remain in achieving sustainable development on the Africa continent ..."

I. United Nations HLPF/ EASG – June 2012 resolutions and outcomes; "future we want[2]" and in specific here is resolution number 183 concerning *Africa; "183 ... While we acknowledge that some progress has been made towards the fulfilment of international commitments related to Africa's development needs, we emphasize that significant challenges remain in achieving sustainable development on the continent".*

II. Mother Language core-inclusion in school curriculum has always and intentionally been left out to undermine Africa Origin of Civilization! Which brings us back to the question; if colonial languages are teachable in Africa, right from nursery school to the highest level of education, then, implementation of SDG4 quality education by 2030 must concern and consequently include Africa Ranykemet language in school core-curriculum, throughout the entire education frame, from the first grade to the highest level of education, without any excuses, just like the United Nations HLPF/ EASG was bossy to bully Africa on FGM a culture Africa practice on in subconsciousness. Ranykemet is the first written down language in the history of man and will forever remain foundational to genuine development, with evidence; Language Comparative Method by Jean Claude Mboli 2010, Paekche's Principle – the Great Secret of Asia by Bayemy Biyick 2014 etc. whatever the case, the implementation of Mother Language UNESCO SDG4 quality education by 2030, must concern Africa spoken languages reunion with (Ranykemet) mother language in Antiquity.

III. The current absence and intentional exclusion of Africa culture history in school core-curriculum is a phenomenon that, among others, Cheikh Anta Diop, Theophile Obenga; 1974, Eric Hobsbawm and Terence Ranger; 1983 and recently Jean Claude Mboli 2010, awaken us to.

---

[2] https://sustainabledevelopment.un.org/index.php?menu=1298

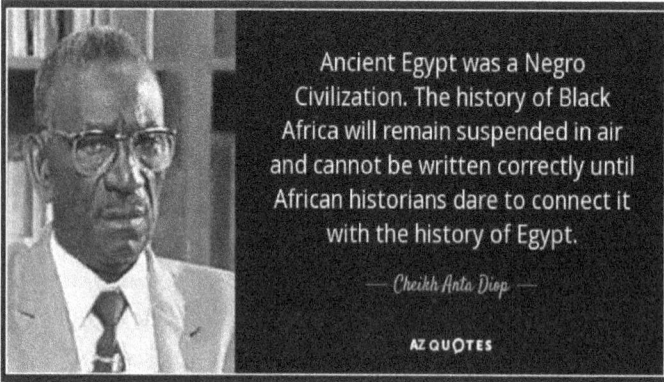

Ancient Egypt was a Negro Civilization. The history of Black Africa will remain suspended in air and cannot be written correctly until African historians dare to connect it with the history of Egypt.

— *Cheikh Anta Diop* —

AZ QUOTES

"When we say that the ancestors of the Blacks, who today live mainly in Black Africa, were the first to invent mathematics, astronomy, the calendar, sciences in general, arts, religion, agriculture, social organization, medicine, writing, technique, architecture; that they were the first to erect buildings out of 6 million tons of stone (the Great Pyramid) as architects and engineers—not simply as unskilled laborers; that they built the immense temple of Karnak, that forest of columns with its famed hypostyle hall large enough to hold Notre-Dame and its towers; that they sculpted the first colossal statues (Colossi of Memnon, etc.)—when we say all that we are merely expressing the plain unvarnished truth that no one today can refute by arguments worthy of the name." **Cheick Anta Diop 1973**

UNDERSTANDING THE IMPACT OF "INVERSION OF TRADITIONS" ON THE AFRICA GRADUATE –

"African politicians, cultural nationalists and, indeed, historians are left with two ambiguous legacies from the colonial invention of traditions. One is the body of invented traditions imported from Europe which in some parts of Africa still exercises an influence on ruling class culture which it has largely lost in Europe itself! As for historians, they have at least a double task. Africa must free themselves from the illusion that the African custom recorded by officials or by many anthropologists is any sort of guide to the African past. But they also need to appreciate how much invented traditions of all kinds have to do with the history of Africa in the twentieth century and strive to produce better founded accounts of them than this preliminary sketch"; **PDF; Eric Hobsbawm and Terence Ranger 1983**

Background

996234843-AVwDHA.Organization's social research Project advocates that Genuine African Development must be Founded on Africa spoken languages re-union with Mother Language in Antiquity. everything else is "inversion of traditions" Facts clearly elaborated in PDF; Eric Hobsbawm and Terence Ranger 1983

This social research Project "Mother Language – Our Common Good – In the Era of SDG4" is a brain child of 996234843-AVwDHA.Org.

Mother Language – Our Common Good – In the Era of SDG4" is **Added Value Project** from 996234843-AVwDHA.Org to **DSD**.

Incentivized from the questions children in the Diaspora ask their parents about their Identity, why is Africa this or that etc. During MDG 2015, a group of Africans in the Diaspora in Norway 2011 – reorganized and revised the articles of association and became registered in the Norway central registry with the name; 996234843-AVwDHA.Organization to meet with the Norwegian Staten white papers; *Jf. Utdrag av Prop 1 S (2011)- Kap. 160.70 Sivilt samfunn ...* that fell into the ears of prepared minds in 996234843-AVwDHA.Org. from 2011 – 2014 the organization created a Project of interest in Saga Africa lore quality time. 2015 the organization Project work advanced to advocating for implementation of Mother Language UNESCO SDG4 quality education by 2030 must concern Africa spoken languages union with mother language in Antiquity.

992634843-AVwDHA.Org is active participant in NGOs based in Norway and NAI; Nordic Africa Institution in Sweden offering courses/ seminars and conferences in Education Development Aid. 992634843-AVwDHA.Org soon came to realize that in Norway NGOs, their education development aid to Africa the questions are not concerned with the absence of Africa spoken languages union with Africa Mother Language in Antiquity and missing from school curriculum core. Now, that is development problem, that is hurting on our part Africa descendants, because in Norwegian NGOs development aid conferences and seminars; every third sentence of given literature, Oral or written, is something about Africa. But there is hardly a word from their mouths about the tools of implementation to advocate for Africa spoken languages unite with mother language in Antiquity.

2).

The Context of Mother Language – Our Common Good from Antiquity or Kemet; known today as "Africa" is the elements of Origin of Civilization or as commonly known as Pharaonic Kemet (km.t)

> "The Spiritual and Scientific founding elements of modern civilization, namely law, knowledge of the matter (mathematics, general and quantum physics, chemistry, medicine, surgery etc.) environment (history, geography, geophysics etc.) and the cosmos (astronomy, cosmology etc.) are rooted in Kemet Civilization"; **Paekche's Principle – the Great Secret of Asia by Bayemy Biyick 2014**

And when the Kemet Spiritual and Scientific founding elements are touched, Maat; the Spiritual Custom, in Kemet Civilization must be touched, Maat was custom until the inversion of Pharaonic Kemet by the Mediterranean population, Western-Asia etc.

Historical Context

The near recent history of Africa adopting foreign languages as official languages, is on a conservative average, at least 3 100 years. Interpreted, this means that Africa has experienced three thousand years of cumulative detachment and the obviously adverse effects of disconnect from the resourcefulness and tools of indigenous Africa that automatically come with healthy connection to indigenous languages. As mentioned earlier, this was and still is an intentional strategy of the concept and principle of inversion of traditions and as well expounded in the Research; "invented of traditions; PDF; Eric Hobsbawm and Terence Ranger 1983".

In contrast to invented tradition of education to Africa, the history of education of Africa Worldview before the Inversion is replete with evidence of the ability, capacity and resourcefulness of African indigenous educational systems and languages to solve Africa problems. For example, African (indigenous) educational systems then, produced graduates who built Modern Civilization; Educational Institutions, Federations, Great Kingdoms and various forms of organizations effectively resolved the challenges and problems of their time with no intervention of foreign development aid. So, what is the effect of this foreign aid in other words inversion of traditions?

The effect of the development aid commonly so called means that genuine and speedy African development is and will always be compromised to distortion and unproductive because the effect of Inversion of Africa turned into Colonialism/ "invented traditions" to Africa and continue to be the case.

But then, in the 21st. century given the tools of implementation; Mother Language UNESCO SDG4 – quality education by 2030 and the tool of mplementation of the United Nations June 2012 resolutions and outcomes "future we want" here in specific resolution 183 concerning Africa … these Tools must take effect here and now. Firstly, to put re-writing of history in check consequently abolish inversion of traditions. The inversion of tradition is a negative complex mechanism embedded with corruption and racism – undoubtedly, the inversion of traditions embedded with racism and corruption is Western Scholars mechanism to coerce the world recognize the Western to be the center of civilization as historical facts continue to unfold in 21st. century. Not only historical facts, even the integration pilot questionnaire in the Western prove to be a questionnaire of guilty conscious incentive. How? The Western integration pilot questionnaire id dedicated to knowing everything about the rest of the World, while hiding who the Western is in terms of the history of their invented traditions. Unfortunately, this forces them to be suspicious people, but the only one they need to be afraid of is the only idea they invented; "inversion of tradition embedded with racism and corruption. Unfortunately, this is the case because of the Western being in denial of common sense truth Africa is the cradle of civilization.

Political, Cultural and Spiritual Context

Missionaries

Foreign missionaries institutionalized the use of their languages in the educational institutions that they built. The output of this educational process was the replacement of the indigenous mind with the foreign. Along with this replacement was the loss of- and or detachment with the resourcefulness, tools and ingenuity that are inherent in indigenous culture of which indigenous language is an integral part. For example, the typical graduate of an African educational system considers everything indigenous as inferior to all things foreign.

So, what is the effect of this graduate to African development to day? this graduate will always consider foreign solutions as the appropriate solutions to Africa problems while being permanently blind to the resourcefulness of indigenous Africa. This is a subject that is covered in depth in the book "African Nationalism" by Ndabaningi Sithole 1959

Additionally, what is the effect of this educational system on the graduate and consequently to indigenous Africa culture? Another equally adverse effect of this educational system on the graduate is the creation of a distorted African identity in all its aspects be it at a personal, social or any other level. This has one its most clear demonstrations in the graduate refusing to embrace his or her African identity. In other words, this educational system produces, consciously or unconsciously, an enslaved mind because the effect the of this education system is to gradually and ultimately detach its graduates from their indigenous identity, culture, language and all the other resources and tools that are inherent in the indigenous culture.

The Spiritual context

Another, just as cruel, adverse effect of this educational system is a graduate who by virtue of detachment from the indigenous culture is consequently divorced from the spiritual resources inherent in the culture. In other words, this graduate is Spiritually powerless because the inclination, consciously or otherwise, but mostly unconsciously, is to embrace the adopted tradition or religion which is simply imitation of indigenous religions; "inversion of traditions – something Eric Hobsbawm and Terrance Rangers explain very well in "inversion of traditions PDF 1983".

Historically, indigenous Africa education systems strengthened the connection of the students to the Spiritual resource inherent in the culture. This ensured that the graduates were well prepared to be resilient in weathering the inevitable tests of life that come in the form of life's hardships. This is not the case of the typical graduate of the current African education system. Because the inclination is to look for help from outside Africa. sadly, this is the case whether that graduate is in or outside Africa.

Africa's education system must produce resilient graduates. Therefore, it is the strongly held argument of this social research that, to produce a graduate that is resilient, Africa's education system requires Africa Worldview to produce a graduate who is resilient.

 it is imperative that the implementation of these tools below,

- Mother Language UNESCO SDG4 quality education by 2030 and
- the United Nations June 2012 resolutions; "future we want[3]"

---

[3] https://sustainabledevelopment.un.org/index.php?menu=1298

15

Colonialism –

With colonialism came the adoption of foreign languages as official languages of respective Africa countries at the expense of advancement of indigenous language as official languages. This was an intentional strategy to dis-empower Africa from the inbuilt resourcefulness that comes with a healthy attachment from Mother language to daughter languages. This is a subject that is covered in depth in the book "African Nationalism" by Ndabaningi Sithole 1959

Development aid

How development aid of education in Africa works to the exclusion of Africa culture in Africa. Active participation in courses/ seminars and conferences in global north, soon one comes to realize that, the Africa adjustment to foreign to Africa commonly will lead to Africa self-destruction, because their education development aid to Africa the questions are not concerned with the absence of Africa spoken languages union with Mother Language in Antiquity and missing from school core-curriculum. This is development problem! That is hurting on our part Africa descendants, because that conditions Africa to detach herself from her authentic and ancestral identity, give-up on who Africa is – while adapting to who the foreigner is. The technical advancement of Africa education and development should be based on Africa Worldview, so that Africa is crystal clear about the concept "to receive" opposed to development aid education to Africa –

But is the development aid a bad idea? In Africa Worldview what is to receive?

"Historical Africa; "to receive", is to bless and be blessed for there is an assumption that there is plenty from where it is coming from. And so, by receiving, you enable that the gift within them to grow bigger, and to flow better. And so, you are giving them a blessing, while blessing yourself. And so, to receive is a blessing... Now, "to take" is different. Taking means that there is an assumption that you do not have enough! So, and therefore, you must fight for every space, regardless of whether there is enough or not. It is as if the world owes to you. Therefore, you must help yourself by imposing your self-styled give to others. Whether the others are willing or not. And even when we examine the analogy of receiving verses the analogy of taking these are completely different. Right, let us experiment on it – how do you receive? Your hand opens to receive. On the other hand, to take your hand folds into a fist so there is almost a force that goes with taking" **Sobonfu Somé**

Evidently from the above we can see this Project meaning on development aid must come from Africa Principles and as Deity Sobonfu teaches.

Historical Africa is where mother language our common good and the birth of knowledge happened, and the place to go back to for a rebirth of knowledge. In the era of SDG – it will be development jeopardy for Africa if Africa spoken languages remain dis-attached from mother language in Antiquity and are not as part of the School core-curriculum.

996234843.-AVwDHA.Org., in the era of SDG2030 participating in Norway and Swedish NGOs education development Aid seminars and conferences, they mostly put emphasis on the other 15 SDGs but not on SDG-4 and SDG-10? Now, what is wrong with SDG-4 and SDG-10?

Consequently, in the era of SDG it is best for Africa emphasis on information sharing on how Africa spoken languages reunion with Africa culture history matters because;

- ▢ Africa spoken languages are intentionally dis-attached from Africa Mother Language in Antiquity consequently, not a core in school curriculum, and
- ▢ It is not wise to study either Africa spoken languages without studying Africa mother language in Antiquity or vice versa. But –
- ▢ There is no way Africa can see this if Africa Education and Development is tailored from cultures outside Africa, because this mainly what NGOs do, bring development aid education to Africa.

Thanks to the use of search engines, such as Google, it was learnt that our organization's Topic of concern discovered other organizations and groups with an interest in Africa History Studies – this is how we connected to peer videos of "conversation with Mboli – comparative method; Mboli 2010" and it was in this way we discovered more Africa Africanists and Afrocentric engaged in Africa History studies in Antiquity. Based on what they had to offer, and our interest in doing information seminars, on Africa spoken languages reunion with Mother Language in Antiquity, we looked at the monetary resources the organization has at hand, made up our minds 2017 to transfer the monies spent on annual reports and annual financial reports to the Norwegian authorities. Will benefit the organization better if we sponsor small Africa groups in On-line Studies in Classic Studies, which will mobilize more Africans to become participants in Afrocentric Discussion groups, where we Propose and argue; Africa spoken languages cannot be taught without re-union with mother language in Antiquity! Meanwhile, the organization also mobilizes partners in home countries to come and join in promoting the Africa spoken languages re-union with Africa History in Antiquity. Since 2016 our organization has introduced small groups of people to do

Online Studies in Seshew mdw nTr royal scribes in Divine Words. This has enabled our Organization and partners in Africa History Studies to demonstrate what we, descendants of Africa, need to do to contribute to bridging the gap between Africa spoken languages reunion with mother language in Antiquity.

This is possible to do if we become many advocating implementations of SDG-4 and SDG-10. IN THE ERA OF SDG, moreover, 2018 our organization got to register to be in that number of DSD Stakeholder because, in the Diaspora we must prove what we explore in the best interest of development in Africa. But not only, humanity; we must become members of a new race, overcoming petty prejudice, owing our ultimate alliance not to nations but to fellow humans – and as our organization logo symbolize man in society, we are all youths and children in mind who must continue to learn about where we are coming from if we must forward march as civilized beings! Consequently, humanity must become more courageous, greater in spirit, larger in outlook if we are to understand who we are to each other by letting the veil of ignorance fall!

Birth of knowledge

Africa Cradle of Civilization. Africa in Antiquity is where early man gave birth to knowledge – aided by the Eye-Mind coordination. The Eye-Mind coordination was early man's road map in exploration and migration. Early man kept on moving and establish sister cultures in this Great Nation Mother-Earth. Early-man made Historical journey to migrate nTr - the home of plenty, go out there in the emptiness, explored, but Early-man made up his mind and never went back to nTr this is how the history goes according to the evolutionary side of the history on the one hand. On the other hand, is the Bible history on the word of God – the Bible says; and then the Lord God sent Adam on Earth. But when Adam felt lonely, he made a U-turn to the Lord God to ask for someone to keep him company. Then Lord God gave Eve to help Adam with glory to go live in Paradise multiply and fill Mother Earth and have dominion over everything on Earth. These are the two histories about birth of knowledge.

Now, whichever side of the history one may choose, Birth of Knowledge took place long time ago in Africa. Whether one want to relay on the evolution history, or the Word of God written in the Bible. Both Histories took place in Africa. what divides these two histories is the time period and below are some references;

> "the long chronology (based on the available data provided by the Kemetic priest Herodotus and Manetho; place the beginning at ca. 17 000 years BCA). And the short chronology of modern are

*obligated to admit that by 4245 BCA. Kemet had already invented the Calendar (which necessarily needed or requires thousands of years to develop)"; **Diop 1973**.*

Now, meanwhile Kemetic priest Herodotus and Manetho; place the beginning at ca. 17 000 years BCA - Historical Bible begins with Abraham the father of the Bible History, Abraham was born in present day Iran moved to Africa to drink from the fountain of birth of knowledge and then started documenting the Bible 2000 BCA. Consequently, it is from such information we come to learn how birth of knowledge happened and from which Re-birth of knowledge becomes common law.

You must get history right; "inversion of traditions" is not custom/ common law. On the other hand, a rebirth of knowledge is custom/ common law.

Rebirth of knowledge

- Rebirth of knowledge is a custom.
- Renaissance is a custom.
- What a True Judge in the courtroom does is Custom.

Custom or common law must not be confused or interchanged with "tradition" –

- The wig and gown the judge wears in court is tradition
- Napoleon sitting on Pharaonic Throne is tradition

"Tradition" in this instance is the institutionalized; the ritualized surrounding their substantial action; Eric Hobsbawm and Terence Rangers; PDF – inversion of traditions 1983.

> ("Eric Hobsbawm and Terence Ranger 1983; refers to modern societies and that includes, the region Europe and Nordic as Traditional Societies. The object and characteristic of traditions in those societies, including invented ones, is seen how inconsistence or invariance show off. The past, real or invented, to which they refer imposes fixed (normally formalized) practices, such as repetition. In modern societies, rituals are Traditions! In short; rituals in modern societies are responses to novel situations which take the form of reference to old situations, or which establish their own. But in most cases these Traditions are the rituals commonly invented, constructed and formally instituted, emerging in a less easily traceable manner within a brief, and dateable period a matter of a few years perhaps- and establishing themselves with great rapidity").

21st. century time is here for Africa graduate Rebirth of knowledge; Right to Sankofa[4] go back to Pharaonic km.t to drink from the Fountain of Knowledge, get the skills right and move forward. The works by hand of early man who Migrated from nTr; the place of plenty to establish society, did it with sense for future generations; you and I, consequently let us all go back to the source to get the skills right, therefore move forward.

Spirit/ spiritual – be conscious of

Teacher Sobonfu Somé; INTIMACY OF SPIRIT PAGE. 13 (BOOK 1997)

> *"When the indigenous people talk about Spirit, they are basically referring to the life force in everything. For instance, you might refer to the spirit in an animal. That is, the life force in that animal, which can help us to accomplish our life purpose and maintain our connection to the Spirit World. The Spirit of the human being is the same way. In our tradition, each of us is seen as Spirit that has taken the form of the Human body to carry out a purpose. Spirit is the energy that helps us connect, that helps us see beyond our racially limited parameters, and helps us in ritual and connecting with the ancestors. Ancestors are also referred to as Spirit"*: **Sobonfu Somé 1997**

With this short introduction to the Intimacy of Spirit, let the reader here be introduced to the 1974 happening, where the Spirit Energy Force move Cheikh Anta Diop and Theophile Obenga in UNESCO-Cairo conference to confront the narrative that Africa is not the originators of civilization –

"Egyptian Civilization is in fact Africa Civilization; Negroid origin – however parodical this may seem. We are not used to, we are not accustomed in fact to endow modern Africa or the early man in Africa with too much intelligence, or even with enough intellect to make the first discoveries necessary for civilization! Yet there is not a single community in interior Africa that has not possessed and does not still poses at least one of those discoveries" **Diop 1973**

As it was earlier mentioned that; inversion of tradition embedded with racisms and corruption must be dealt with and abolished. Here this Project argue; inversion of tradition embedded with racisms and corruption should be abolished through the implementation of SDG-10 reducing inequality within a nation and among countries by 2030. How? Well, inversion of tradition embedded with racisms and corruption is ongoing because Research is one sided, whereby global north wants to know everything in global south but not any

---

[4] Sankofa is a word in Akan language in Ghana it is also a name of a bird and literary means go back and get.

one to know everything about global north. So, by global south actively become researchers in global north. This is the social engine that will work for the abolition of inversion of tradition embedded with racisms and corruption, because it is for this reason that explorers from global north give themselves scientific names but name the rest of us other names like; migrants, asylum seeker etc. but both global north and global south come from equal incentives as explorers. Both explorers depend on the same resources and have the same needs in common –

- The fact that they both keep moving back and forth to live, or work/ research outside their native homes – they are both explorers!
- Both base on the fundament of eye-sight – mind coordination to explorer/ argue; choosing freely to enter to live work/ research across borders in search of wisdom! By the way, the mere moment one sets foot off native land; his / her horizon rises no matter to what degree therefore,
- Either one is working in native land, or else; he or she is in the Diaspora.
- Indeed, we must all develop our skills to do effective research to beat down inversion of tradition embedded with racisms and corruption through the implementation of SDG4 and SDG10

Think of United Nation June 2012 resolutions and outcome; "the future we want" …

Resolution 183 … Africa "183. While we acknowledge that some progress has been made towards the fulfilment of international commitments related to Africa's development needs, we emphasize that significant challenges remain in achieving sustainable development on the continent".

Africa Must Need from United Nations June 2012 resolutions and outcome; "future we want" - resolution number 183 concerning Africa Needs … And with the unfolding Mother Language UNESCO SDG4 quality education by 2030 implementation of SDG4 for Africa must be Africa spoken languages reunion with mother language in Antiquity and a part of School Core-Curriculum such that this becomes the common denominator by 2022 whoever wants to enter to live, work/ research in Africa must have a certificate in at least general knowledge of the above. So far; we know of and participate in USA based On-line Studies engaging Africa Classic Studies; we do 3 – 5 hours information seminars and then top-up with On-line studies in Africa history Studies for 2 hours one day of the week for 12 weeks. Therefore, we think that with regards to United Nations resolutions and outcome "future we want", this must be a Calling is not to fall aback, this must be a Calling to keep striving for. 2018 the organization again reorganized to become initiative stakeholders in DSD therefore, we try to keep communication with United Nations DSD active. We are; 996234843-AVwDHA.Org short-form for Added Value with Diaspora Home-Away is "Africa" volunteer organization based and registered in Norway. 26th October 2018 sent an Email to DSD *Knowledge Platform* dsd@un.org – for Partnerships for DSD - initiative registered #27717 (Ref #156732) and was responded to; Thank you for registering a multi-stakeholder partnership/voluntary commitment in the Partnerships for DSD online platform. Here our job is to bring forward the Added Value as DSD request of. Were we hereby confirm the book title; "in the are of DSD-SDG2030" is Africa inquiry to UN-HLPF/ EASG about the June 2012 resolutions "future we want" …?

3).

Details from the Authors and Literatures on which this objective is founded –

- Africa Origin of Civilization, Myth or reality; Diop 1973

    Birth of Knowledge; Africa Cradle of Civilization –

    throughout in Antiquity as well as modern world, Africa remains the classic land where the contemporary world goes on Pilgrimage to drink at the Fountain of scientific, religious, moral and social knowledge, the most ancient knowledge of mankind will forever acknowledge; Africa origin of Civilization; **Diop 1973**

    Rebirth of knowledge – is Sankofa, go back to the source of birth of knowledge to get the Skills –
    - ➢ *the Persians 525 BC went back to Africa Nile Valley to get the skills right*
    - ➢ *Alexander 333 BC, the Greco Romans with Julius Caesar 50 BC,*
    - ➢ *the Arabs; seventh century*
    - ➢ *the Turks in the sixteenth century*
    - ➢ *the French with Napoleon and then the English at the end of the nineteenth century …*
    - ➢ *Nevertheless, it would long continue to initiate the younger Mediterranean peoples; Greco-Roman among others into the Enlightenment of Civilization from the source; Africa in Antiquity.*
    - ➢ *Throughout in Antiquity as well as modern world, Africa remains the classic land where the contemporary world goes on Pilgrimage to drink at the Fountain of scientific, religious, moral and social knowledge, the most ancient knowledge of mankind will forever acknowledge;* Africa origin of Civilization – **Myth or Reality; Cheikh Anta Diop 1973**.

- Hobsbawm and Ranger 1983.

    "Even if agents of invented traditions codify and promulgate tradition, thereby transforming flexible custom into hard prescription. All this is part of the history of European ideas, but it is also very much part of the history of modern Africa. These complex processes must be understood before a historian can arrive at any understanding of the particularity of Africa before colonialism; many African scholars as well as many European Africanists have found it difficult to free themselves from the false models of colonial codified African 'tradition'. **PDF Eric Hobsbawm and Terence Ranger 1983.**

- Jean Claude Mboli: Language Comparative Method 2010

    Comparative Method of Jean Claude Mboli 2010 here we show extract diagram from his teaching how language came to man in Africa, and how language evolve in time and space? It is a

Francophone spoken research book. For those of us who happen to be Anglophone spoken, we can easily participate by following the You tube peer video; "Conversation with Jean Claude Mboli himself live"; one of the premier linguists in our period of life time, is one of those dedicated people who reconstruct the sister language genetic relationships with the mother language in Antiquity.

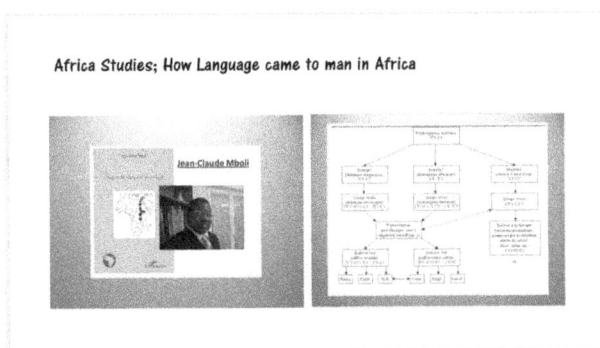

Africa Studies; How Language came to man in Africa

Besides the literature from the book title; Africa origin of civilization by Cheick Anta Diop, to know about the conversation with Mboli was through online studies by among others two linguistics; Asar Imhotep and Wudjau Iry Maat who with Mr. Mboli. The two dedicate their quality time forth and back from comparative method to genetically sister languages of a common mother language in Antiquity.

Africa cradle of civilization dates to 17 000 years –

"It is generally agreed that 7000 BCE the Sahara had dried up, Equatorial Africa was probably a forest zone to dense to attract men. Consequently, the last Africa populations who had lived in the Sahara, presumably left it to migrate towards the upper Nile … whatever the case, it was from the gradual adaptation to the new living conditions which nature assigned to those various Africa populations that the oldest phenomenon of civilization came about! This civilization called Egyptian in our contemporary life, developed for a long time in the early Cradle; then it slowly descended the Nile Valley to continue spread elsewhere. This circle of civilization, the longest in history presumably lasted for 10 000 years. This is a reasonable compromise between the long chronology (based on the data provided by Kemetic priests, Herodotus and Manetho place the beginning at 17 000 B.C) and the short chronology of the modern for the latter are obligate to admit that by 4245 B.C Kemet had already invented the Calendar (which necessary requires the passage of thousands of years" page 22 – Africa Origin of Civilization Myth or Reality; Cheikh Anta Diop 1973

It is inevitable to keep referring to inspiring works of Diop. because his works is the incentive Africa in the Diaspora continue to explorer and gather information, moving back and forth between native countries and foreign countries in self-help Africa to gain conscious of knowledge how the Nile Valley Civilization matters for Africa spoken languages continuity Weave and Embroider and we will show from pictures 3 – 5 here below.

 If truth be told; there is a researcher in all humanity because in time and space once the eye has caught sight automatically mind starts the race to go over there and explore … Perhaps, it is not fair to term people from global south; migrants, asylum seekers etc. when in fact whether one is from global south or global north pretty much both peoples are incentivized from the coordination of eye sight – mind race to go there; explorer, gain the knowledge in search for. Both use the coordination of eye sight – mind exploration. The Goal is equal and that is, to raise horizon in development. Their bodies live in the Diaspora, but their minds are always at home in the country of origin, unlike early man who migrated nature and entered emptiness, explored; created civilization – made up his mind never to go back to nTr! Early man is the only one who qualifies to be migrant. Modern people can only go by the term "in the Diaspora"

Migration started and ended with early man in antiquity. Consequently, modern people simply do the same thing – move forth and back in the Diaspora – for a rebirth of knowledge, a custom a common law, not tradition.

"The invented traditions[5] of African societies whether invented by the whites or by Africans themselves in response - distorted the past but became in themselves realities through which a good deal of colonial encounter was expressed";
PDF – invented traditions by Eric Hobsbawm and Terrance Ranger 1983

nTr, what do the three consonants nTr are stand for or tell?

The three consonants are from Ranykemet language "Speech of Kemet" transliteration God – infinite. Better still nTr is Kemet Temple Future icon R8 cloth on pole. It is usual to see R8 combined with S43 mdw = "words", the Kemet "S" Sign list for Regalia and Clothing. Then the combination of S43 and R8 in Speech of Kemet reads out either as "mdw nTr" or Medew Netcher. The combination of these two words mdw nTr carries the meaning of expressions of the divine, divine expressions – communication of nature and existence; **Wudjau Iry Maat 2015**

[5] http://psi424.cankaya.edu.tr/uploads/files/Hobsbawm_and_Ranger_eds_The_Invention_of_Tradition.pdf

Africa Classic Studies teach; the three consonants; nTr is "rot word" transliteration from Kemet Hieroglyphs to spoken languages for example the English language, whereby the English wore "nature" comes from the Ranykemet rot word nTr. In Africa spoken languages, the rot word nTr is alive and well, living on as words "Ntore" "Ntere". These words are the same word coming from the rot word "nTr" in Antiquity. Not surprising all three words; nTr ↔ Ntore ↔ Ntere refer to the word ↔ God - infinite. The vowels may vary but the consonants remain constant! Which again is correct because Early Man in Antiquity who wrote these messages on papyrus reeds and the Walls of the Pyramids, they did not write vowels of any word. For them the word nTr – God – infinite and coming from infinite. If you will happen to join studies in "Seshew mdw nTr" is where one learns why the Studies are called Studies of "divine words". commonly it is known that the Scribes or authors in the Nile Valley in Africa studying the sounds or sound waves in nTr or "nature" as we call it in English language. "nTr" is secrete; Divine!

Scholars in Ranykemet, the first written down language 5 000 years ago by Royal scribes in sSw mdw nTr say that; the Royal scribes in sSw mdw nTr did not write down vowels in any word, they only wrote down consonants to stand in for sound-waves; the secret of scribing Divine sound-waves.

Earlier above we have learnt from Teacher Sobonfu Some` about the intimacy of spirit. Here spirit energy forces/ sound-waves was major tool for Early man to study and understand the energy movement in the Universe. For Spirit; the energy force movement can turn into various forms. Spirit is the energy transformation into everything; energy can transform into sound waves, into minerals, plant, animals, Humans, and Events. But that is another book, another level of education. Here the objective is messenger of truth advocating for implementation of SDG-4 quality education by 2030; for Africa spoken languages reunion with Africa culture history in Antiquity. that is not too much for Africa to ask for. That is Africa asking for Transparence, Accountability and Legitimacy contract with development aid education to Africa, that is Africa asking for a common denominator; Mother Language for Africa and foreign investments to Africa, must be based on Africa Worldview from mother language our common good.

On the notice from United Nations June 2012 resolution 183 – Africa, United Nations EASG have everything to gain by advocating for Africa spoken languages are reunited with Mother language in Antiquity. And this is to say; the school curriculum is the rightful plant form to study History of early man. History of man must be brought out and become reflected clearly in spoken languages. Because, as revealed by Eric Hobsbawm and Terrance Ranger PDF 1983; inversion of traditions are rituals commonly invented, constructed and formally instituted … now that brings to our attention how invented traditions/ corruption and racism are the samething! "Invented traditions/ corruption and racism" must be scandal in the history of missionaries – colonialism followed by the running 60 years of development aid education to Africa; if United Nations is not going to be in the favor of in the era of DSD -DSG4 quality education by 2030

By Africa spoken languages union with mother language in Antiquity and apart of school curriculum. Means that Africa will live a conscious life, go about their business as usual but this time round, they can explain and define what they are doing. That is essential for education and development. Does not mean that Africa will stop working and being social or sign for alliances with NGOs. It simply means Africa will move out of the position of development aid/ client, to a position of development aid partner!

If we must recall from the MDG 2015. Global north used to demand for Transparence; Accountability; legitimacy – using the same principle it should quickly make sense to United Nation/ HLPF/ EASG how Africa having knowledge of self is global south being equal with global north in Transparence; Accountability; legitimacy when dealing with development aid partners. Transparences; Accountability and legitimacy must not be only be in the interest of counting monies of the development aid donor nations! This must also concern the scandals surrounding why donor nations do hold Africa spoken languages dis-attached from mother language un antiquity.

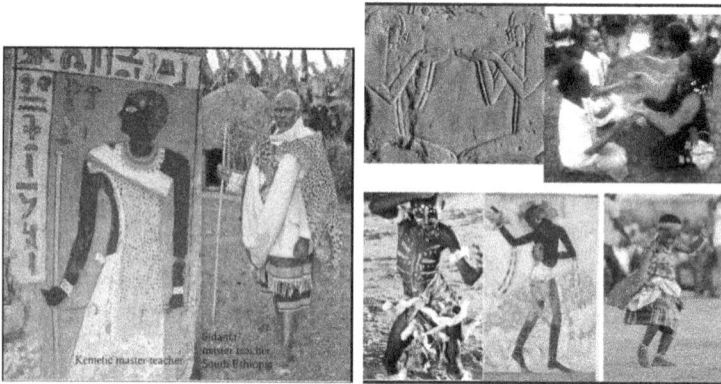

Picture 3 – 4 see footnote. Pic.4 is extract from one of Africa struggling with Africa studies in school corridor especially linguistics dedication to do On-line studies to cause awareness. Picture 5 is extract from Asar Imhotep collections. Many of us in modern Africa see it and can name it but beyond that we do not know or cannot explain the concept in there. Picture 5 points to the ox-tail carried by the Pharaoh on his tablet 4000 BCE, the Pharaoh and the Priests carried ox-tails Asterisk of Social-Political Moral Power. This is still born in modern Africa ceremonies and cultural functions unfortunately modern Africa is subconscious of her own history and culture because of a development aid education with strategy to disorient Africa spoken languages from mother language in Antiquity! Modern Africa can hardly explain where Africa is coming from. That is absurd! Implementation of SDG4 must make way for Africa people to learn about what they do with clear consciousness, because culture history matters. Because it is pointless to hide who/ what and where Africa is in mind.

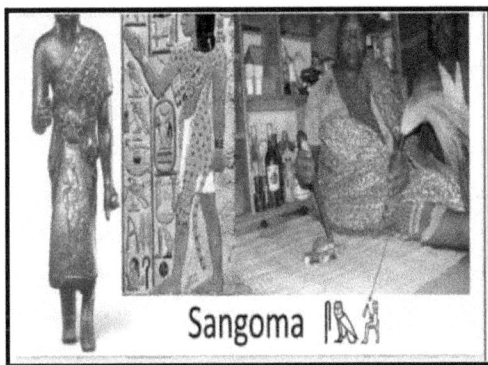

Sangoma

Africa legacy of relating spirit form from related spirit forms to enhance political, religious and social moral power should be studied in Africa and explained to African to know the concepts therein, so that people do the right things the right way and in the correct manner. That is Custom. Take an example; Africa association of the Lion Spirit form of power with the spirit form of speed, spirit form of Leadership, and then crown a Ruler/ Deity/ Priest with those social moral powers – there is nothing evil or voodoo in there until some intellectual acrobatic comes around to disorient a people from Cradle of Civilization; Social-Political Moral Power. Every important-decision making building should be surrounded with social-political moral symbols – as Custom not tradition.

Pictures 3 to 4 are taken from Prof; Mwafrica Mkenya; comparing African Spiritual dress code from 4000 years to modern Africa?

> "In Africa[6], therefore, the whole apparatus of invented school and professional and regimental traditions became much more starkly a matter of command and control than it was within Europe itself".

---

[6] http://psi424.cankaya.edu.tr/uploads/files/Hobsbawm_and_Ranger_eds_The_Invention_of_Tradition.pdf

The relevance of rebirth of knowledge – a custom for forwardness is relevant in the era of SDG4 to take away the regimental traditions a matter of command and control as stated here above.

The East Africa Nile Valley heritage is the history of man. It is all mankind's right to, get the skill right from School Curriculum Core. The era of SDG is fit for information era preceded from the turn of the 20th. century with messages of truth moving messengers like 1974; Diop and Obenga in UNESCO-Cairo Conference, causing awareness, history of man is in wrong hands trying to rewrite history!

In the era of SDG, we must be conscious of the messengers of truth; Bob Marley from the ghetto, 1974 - Diop and Obenga in UNESCO-Cairo Conference, Hobsbawm and Terence Ranger; inversion of traditions 1983 etc. are messengers of truth provoking the spread of invented traditions. While advocating for indigenous people to perform custom they are experts of! The Media, the air-waves – are also messengers of truth, if one has basic knowledge of what is educative in social media. Resilient organization like 996234843-AVwDHA.Org from Africa and researching in global north, in the era of information are also messengers of truth. 21st. century is indeed Re-birth of knowledge era. A common law is once again Calling. The Spirit of message of truth is transforming from one body to another body. So, why not all put on social research to beat down the inversion of traditions embedded with racism and corruption.

Prof: Patrice Lumumba Otieno; lecture "Africa at the Dinner table"– Kigali 14th. May 2018

"Africa at the Dinner table" speech by Prof: Patrice Lumumba Otieno – Kigali 14th. May 2018, he speaks on how the Elite Conceptual West prove to be intellectual acrobatics! He goes on to say; the Elite Conceptual West does not want to see stability in specific regions of the world. They plan strategy to see to it that there is constant conflict in those regions because conflict is a major industry for the elite conceptual western. He goes on to say; today if you look at South Sudan and the many peace conferences that are being conducted there. But if you ask who supplies the weapons of war? It is the Elite Conceptual West. To protect the Neo Colonialists Project to punish to the core contemporary Africa for the reason no one should learn Africa is the Cradle of Civilization? The Neo-colonial Project requires that Africa must remain in the sphere of the influence Elite in Conceptual West invented traditions.

4).

Case Studies are ostensible in this Project's case; to help illuminate the phenomenon; "why is Africans struggling with Mother Language Studies in School Corridors"? short list here below. Consequently, there are three identified research questions and five assumptions –

Identified research questions and assumptions

RESEARCH QUESTION 1:

Mother Language UNESCO SDG4 quality education by 2030 is here, SDG10 reducing inequality within a nation and among countries is here – why is Africa struggling with Africa History in Antiquity studies in school corridors?

Assumption 1:

If Africa provoking implementation of SDG4 will be sabotaged, still Africa must free themselves from the illusion that the African custom recorded by officials or by many anthropologists is any sort of guide to the African past. Moreover, ongoing colonialism to Africa, cleverly use the development aid mechanism to coerce the Africa graduates keep distorted from their identity, culture, language and all the other resources and tools that are inherent in the indigenous culture. Because the effect of this development aid of educational system to Africa on the graduate and consequently to indigenous Africa culture? Another equally adverse effect of development aid educational system on the graduate is the creation of a distorted African identity in all its aspects be it at a personal, social or any other level.

Assumption 2:

If colonial languages to Africa are teachable from pre-primary to the highest level of education. Truth is, Mother Language in Antiquity is likewise teachable from pre-primary to every level of Africa continuity! No more excuses and that brings us to research question number 2 –

RESEARCH QUESTION 2:

With regards SDG10 reducing inequality within a nation and among countries How serious is the integration question regarding the research question number one in the era of SDG?

Assumption 3

When attending development aid conferences/ seminars, during break time and mingling, it is shocking to meet some researchers from global north have the guts to pull aside participants from African and talk with them in African spoken languages! And if you ask them;

> Question.   "where and how did you learn the language you are speaking"?

> Answer.   while on my Project work in Africa, I teach myself with the help of the natives.

That is signal such researchers are encouraging to learn Africa spoken languages on the streets ... When the right thing to do is advocate for Africa spoken languages reunion with mother language through implementation of SDG4/ SDG10 and with regards to June 2012 United Nations; future we want ... resolution number 183 concerning what Africa need ... so that Africa spoken languages unite with mother language and, a part of school curriculum core. So that, self-studies are based on school curriculum, so that indigenous people advance knowledge of self and become resilient to invented traditions.

Assumption 4

It is important to make an inquiry in United Nation HLPF/ EASG; what is Scientific and or Human Rights in taking pictures of people in global south portraying endless misery and backwardness. and repeatedly share these pictures between NGOs? Meanwhile, we see the problem of self-hate happening, psychological self-hate problem remain dig deep and painful? Humanitarian declaration cannot be called for but keep coercing a people to dissociate from Historical Human Culture in Antiquity. The essential factor is; during the era of DSD-SDG affirm a people retrace their history in Antiquity.

RESEARCH QUESTION 3:

Do you think that Africa States and Governments are to blame for Africa spoken languages disoriented from mother language in antiquity?

Assumption 5.

Contemporary Africa States and Governments are the product of invented traditions education to Africa. Unless, Africa introduces Africa Worldview in school core-curriculum. The leadership in Africa will remain a client of donor nations and as we expounded in –

African politicians, cultural nationalists and, indeed, historians are left with two ambiguous legacies from the colonial invention of traditions. One is the body of invented traditions imported from Europe which in some parts of Africa still exercises an influence on ruling class culture which it has largely lost in Europe itself! As for historians, they have at least a double task. Africa must free themselves from the illusion that the African custom recorded by officials or by many anthropologists is any sort of guide to the African past. But they also need to appreciate how much invented traditions of all kinds have to do with the history of Africa in the twentieth century and strive to produce better founded accounts of them than this preliminary sketch"; **PDF; Eric Hobsbawm and Terence Ranger 1983**

5).

This Project finds it marvel development aid education to Africa from missionaries ↔ colonialism ↔ development aid of education to Africa, do not mind about integration in Africa spoken languages union with mother language in Antiquity is fundamental to Africa development. That is absurd! Must be brought to the attention of Africa States and Governments and inquiry in United Nations; HLPF/ EASG/ DSD …

"To receive" verse "to take" must be very well understood following Teacher/ Deity; Sobonfu Some alerts us to become conscious, to receive is a blessing … but "to take is different.
But again, history will judge you by your actions in life, not what others did to you. Living example is invented traditions embedded with corruption and racism these are traceable back to the Authors - according to; January 2018 Racism debate by Johan Galtung Q and A; listen to minutes; 3;20 – 3;34 https://www.youtube.com/watch?v=LcEDSmm56mc "Abrahamic civilization is in conflict with itself" …

NUPI; Oslo Norway; Foreign Affairs Debate 15th March 2018 minutes; 4;45 – 5;28 level of general knowledge production, we have had a period of 200 years where knowledge production has been circulating about Europe, Europe claim to be the central of knowledge …
https://www.youtube.com/watch?v=VUZ_-bUrTNs

For Africa if Africa spoken languages reunions with Mother language in Antiquity is a part of School Curriculum Core, will be effective, because there are four resources in Africa for the advantage of implementation of Africa spoken languages reunion with mother language in Antiquity for effective results;

The four resources are –

- Africa population
- Africa spoken languages
- Africa media
- Africa school curriculum.

Africa media – commonly both TV program, Radio etc. must create space at least 2 X 2 hours a week to inform Africa population causing awareness how Africa was conditioned to forget Africa History. Importantly, resource number four! Africa schools need to divide the time Africa uses on colonial languages to equal the time Africa needs to learn to read and write Ranykemet the firs written down language in Antiquity the true documentation of mother language our common good. This is how Africa population is going to be guided to knowledge of how language came to man in Africa. Africa It is Africa time to do custom – go back to the source and get the skills right to move forward!

> As for Africa historians, they have at least a double task; to free themselves from the illusion that the African custom recorded by officials or by many anthropologists is any sort of guide to the African past. But they also need to appreciate how much invented traditions of all kinds have to do with the history of Africa in the twentieth century and strive to produce better founded accounts of them than this preliminary sketch; Eric Hobsbawm and Terence Ranger PDF 1983

Ethnical Problems; Ethnical tragedy 13th May 2018 under way this Social Research

Sun-God Shines Light of Enlightenment Every Day, let Otim too
Nowell Christian-Merry Onyee; MSc. Management 2016/2017
University of Bath

Dissertation

"A Strategic Analysis Concerning the Competitive Relationship Between Full Service Network Airlines and Low-Cost Carriers in the European Airlines Industry

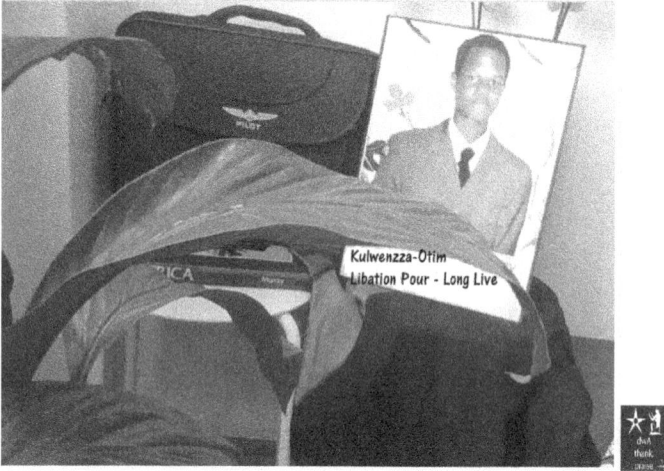

Kulwenzza-Otim
Libation Pour - Long Live

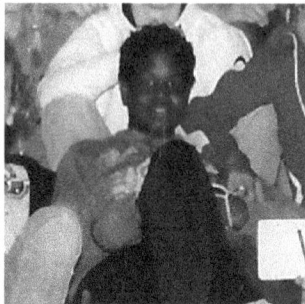

14th. May 2018 sad news reached Oslo, Norway that son from Africa soil was found lifeless in London, United Kingdom. From the given statement given by the Tåsen – Oslo reverend, it was not difficult to see how the 2015 – 2018 behavior in the Norwegian high circles in the international politics is behind the death of African-Norwegian youth in picture; 6 – 10 above. Corruption/ racism embedded in invented traditions is the only reason Norway wanted this young man's life taken, to eliminate evidence, forgetting the fact that no man is an Island. 21st. century exposes Africa to the Authors ↔ literature and case studies to be encouraged to think objectively on Africa education ↔ Sustainable development goals ↔ "future we want". Norway intellectual Acrobatic took away life of Youth in photos 6 – 10 here above. He was in that number of Africa Youth who Carry Our Promise for Tomorrow … Norway intellectual Acrobatic were very careful to leave no evidence, now that the evidences are as clear as day light. Norway as a family member of Elite Conceptual Western, their next move will be to put on weapons of mass destruction to protect their own crime. I think the best thing is to apologize, pay the monies Norway killed this youth for to make things better rather than enemy creating continuity. The history of inversion of traditions is not impressive even to you the Authors of invented traditions! Evidence; January 2018 Oslo Norway put on a Racism Debate lead by Johan Galtung; Norwegian Senior Researcher in "PRIO"; Peace Research Institute Oslo. With reference to the United Nations Call for Initiative Contribution to SDGs - 996234843-AVwDHA.Org (Africa Diaspora Org) representative participated in this Debate with comments and questions regarding SDGs pschological time and space. On that notice, the audience worked out feeling inspired to hear from Africa with such Knowledge and Spirit!

The By the way, it is rare to see a global north journalist take an African's picture properly if this African is in panel debate on Global Social questions Debates. This time it happened. But do you know what? By January 2019 that recording was removed from Media.

6).

This social research began with an Introduction, the Context, the Literatures and Authors, the Case Studies, the Findings as the research sees it wise to gather and put in the chapters a head of chapter 6; the discussion here and now. Consciously what goes on in this discussion is founded on genuine procedure, to determine the aim and goal of Africa conscious community struggling with Africa Classic Studies in School Corridors. Firstly, it is necessary to cause clear understanding why Africa is coerced to foreign history of Enslavement, Missionaries, Colonialism, ongoing development aid of education to Africa. History has come to reveal all the mentioned demarcates themselves as inversion of tradition embedded with racism and corruption. Consequently, what Africa must do is Sankofa; go back and get the skills right if Africa must move forward! The Africa graduate cannot get that education system to develop into a resilient graduet if she or he does not put in efforts to Sankofa, go back to the source to get the Skills right. Africa is home to early man and that should shame anybody who is proud to teach colonial languages intentionally to disorient Africa from continuity of Mother Language the cradle of civilization. A development aid education to Africa that finds it ridiculous to integrate Africa spoken languages reunion with Mother Language in Antiquity and a part of school core-curriculum, is an obstacle to Africa development. This Project work shows that, the answers to the research question 1 should not be complex because the answer is self-explanatory in assumption 1. firstly, if the education development aid of education to Africa was and or is in the best interest for Africa, then why not see the agency of Africa spoken languages union with mother language in Antiquity and a part of Africa school core-curriculum

Truth be told; invented traditions embedded in corruption and racism, are not mechanisms of uneducated peoples. Truth is Invented traditions embedded in corruption and racism is an instrument of scholars, the brains behind colonialism etc.

Now Assumption 2 is self-critique, the teaching and learning colonial languages from the Missionaries ↔ Colonialism ↔ NGOs. We must not fall in the same mistake of assumption 3. Here the goal is to advocate for implementation of SDG4 quality education by 2030, SDG10 reducing inequality within a nation and among countries, in the best interest of June 2012 resolution number 183 concerning Africa needs point of view.

Research question two about Integration; assumption 3 reveals the very people of high education/ scholars trusted with development aid projects cannot help to look sideways, after all they claim it is ridiculous for global north to integrate in global south, where they should in fact care to support doing Africa spoken languages union with mother language from school curriculum core. A senior researcher in development aid must be ashamed of him/ herself to pick up Africa spoken languages and boast of speaking the language. Moreover, he or she knows the importance of learning a language from a school curriculum core. Assumption 4 sought out to investigate the relationship between Scientific methods and or Human Rights; the pictures taken by United Nations; share in global north NGOs then spread them everywhere in the media!

Here is some good example to explain how the phenomenon should be understood!

A good Samaritan who is helping to collect monetary resources for a Cancer patient on treatment, put the patient's photograph in what's-up to show how the patient is struggling with the Cancer. This is how one of the comments/ reactions to the good Samaritan;

From Donor to the Samaritan; "Samaritan"; thank you for the information, we appreciate. Can I please, request that you hold back on sending the patient's photo of the tumor every time you send information about the patient, please. Personally, I find it too graphic to keep seeing.

Samaritan to Donor; Absolutely, it is intrusive and offends the patient's confidentiality. Why do I keep sending it then? Desperation. Sorry, I will leave it to that. Thank you.

Likewise, in a good way, please donor nations; can you please spare development aid receiver nations the psychological and physical self-hate pictures you share in the media, it is too graphic.

June 2012 United Nations resolution "future we want"/ resolution number 183; Africa needs among others is Africa, foreign workers and researchers to work under the common denominator where Africa spoken languages united with Africa Mother Language in Antiquity. Humanitarian declaration cannot be called for but keep portraying a people in theme of endless misery, portray in motif of failed nations etc. The essential factor is let a people retrace their history in Antiquity during the era of SDG.

Research question number 3; the case studies in Norway NGOs and NAI of Sweden, reveal that Africa leaders as well as Africa population, we are coerced to think within limits of missionaries and colonial education to Africa, until the upcoming leaders in Africa are taught to think and reason outside the box of invented traditions to Africa. and remember; if we blame them then we must also tell them what they must do differently.

This also clearly came out during in the case study in Norwegian NGOs and NAI of Sweden, of without which it was impossible to see how corruption and racism are embedded in invented traditions education syllabus to Africa. Much effort is put in such alliances even if we know how they dis-orient Africa from working independent of global north education development Aid. Blaming Africa leadership is no better than spend time understanding the cause and effect of invented traditions to Africa. The right thing to do is affirm Africa leadership in Africa Worldview so that Africa transcend and rise;
https://www.youtube.com/watch?v=Q5Gk36pUu1k 28th Nov 2017 Uppsala University Lecture on Africa Poverty; the Prof. said of democratization not working for Africa – true because when talking of Africa progress, it is done putting on the lenses of invented traditions to Africa, rather than talking more for Africa in Africa ... so the inspiration to Africa youths, upcoming leaders in Africa, you should take inspiration from Africa spoken languages union with mother language in Antiquity... This input fell on attentive ears, in the lecture room.

By the way, change will not happen in Africa until Africa Worldview is a part of school curriculum core. Africa must be educated beyond the last 200 years school curriculum, otherwise Africa leadership will continue to make the same mistakes. Modern Africa proposing for regime change of government, makes the same mistake. What needs to change in Africa is the school curriculum. Ask senior chefs; no one changes the test of food by changing the stove! You change the test of food by changing the ingredients.

Limitation – ethical problems

Racism tragedy 13th. May 2018

The ethical problem that the organization this Project work was forced to face is typically corruption/ racism embedded in development aid education to Africa. 14th. May 2018; sad news reached Oslo, Norway that son from Africa soil was found lifeless in London, United Kingdom. It was not difficult to notice where all this was coming from! Obviously by looking in the period 2015 - 2018 Norway cruel behavior to the diseased and his mother tells it all! Yet Norway 2011 came out with the white papers in favor of added value with Diaspora home-little did we know that Norway brought this out only for keeping appearances, while doing cruel things to minorities behind closed doors, like the act of 13th May 2018! The behaviors of Norway to the diseased and his mother are evidence enough to hold Norway suspect number one in the death of this young man. But for the same reason his life was taken is the same reason Norway should have protected the young man's life. The reader here may take a step back, refer to Prof. Patrice Lumumba Otieno points out here above; elite conceptual west does not like to see stability and development in Africa! is the same Norway behavior towards 996234843-AVwDHA.Org even if this organization is registered in the Norwegian central registrar, previously all the obligations and commitments to do development Projects, are fulfilled, documented and with punctual annual reports, no monetary frauds in the organization whatsoever and etc. On their part, Norway on catching sight of an Africa Diaspora Organization in the media 2016 steadily raising, no doubt Norway pulled out the racial card! Undoubtedly this is what invented traditions/ corruption and racism minds hate are good at. The guilt Norway carry from court cases 2016 to date and 2017 -2018 salaries stealing from the mother of the diseased are also evident in the way they respond to the family questions about what happened to their son? This is how Norway has answered since May 2018 –

First question to Norway Police June 2018 was; please is there anything Police can tell us about our beloved? The police look through data on PC, go to back room come back after 30 minutes and the answer was; you know he did not die in Norway, best you go and ask in London UK where he died. In separate letters from the mother to the Norwegian Authorities –

Question 2. In the period 2016 – 2018 Norway brought him to both law court and high court, accused by high ranking Police officer behind closed doors, not allowed any witness. Accused of running away from the Police on the said night. That same night began threats and isolation against his family, from his social milieu, his ethnic Norwegian friend with whom he was the night, he went out to cerebrate his success upon becoming an Aircraft Pilot June 2016.

So, suppose he was with a fellow African not ethnic Norwegian or white for that matter. Would both be brought to Court?

Question 3. Is it usual to hold the accused in Court for all those rounds without any witness(s)? There is no answer from Norwegian authorities – just silence, stiff lips – no answer!

Question 4. Was it by plan or was it a coincidence August 2016 Oslo court put off TV-license - compensation to the mother of Kulwenzza-Otim for bleach of name for the TV-license she had already paid for, to bring the son to the same Court; Oslo Court, or was it calculated steps, typical intellectual acrobat; buying time from the Mother compensation case? That night he was with ethnic Norwegian friend you play intellectual acrobatic to separate the two, bring the black man to court, no witness of his friend with whom the complainant found him cannot stand as witness in this case. And not only in this same connection you throw the mother's TV-license compensation out of court to drag the son in court instead, does that sound like corruption and racism? Because Norway conditioned the son to a fine in high court But, Norway keep quiet about court TV license compensation to the mother, since August 2016 this is 2018, how about that?

There is no answer. The current reactions; dead silence, just stiff lips! The guilty are conscious.

Question 5. How does Norwegian Labor Directorate explain keeping quiet with the mother's salaries? Is it usual to send out documentation of release of outstanding pay from January 2017 to January 2018, but then refuse to deposit the monies in the Bank Account of the receiver?

There is no answer from these Norwegian Authorities, just reaction of dead silence, stiff lips!

Question 6 is it difficult to see the motive behind is Norwegian High circles involved in Kulwenzza-Otim death. Following the evidence of Norwegian authorities causing psychological and physical pain to both mother and son, and evidence all the torture concerns their participating in 996234843-AVwDHA.Org which was created under the guidelines of Jf. Utdrag av Prop 1 S (2011)- Kap. 160.70 Sivilt samfunn …?

Still there no answers! The answers from Norwegian authorities is dead silence, just stiff lips!

Such are the evidences and more; when we look at the 996234843-AVwDHA.Org biography, we see some NGOs Senior Researchers have removed some Seminar video recordings with 996234843-AVwDHA.Org Participation! Norway is suspect number one in the death of Kulwenzza-Otim. To end his life in London UK, is intellectual Acrobatic from Norway authorities in question. Norway intentionally held back monies from the mother to intensify isolation between the mother and son.

But the mother insists it is not over, the monies above mentioned and being held back in Norwegian Court since December 2016 and the monies the Norwegian Labor directorate is holding back from the mother since January to 2017 to Date must be released. To open forensic research in her child's death. the monies will help her to get the chance to enter the alleged scene where her son's life was ended. Importantly, she says; despite the Norwegian intellectual Acrobatic to murder her son to earn him indecent burial ceremony, to amplify self-hate in Black community! Her son's achievements read he was a man of Airforce Cadre as Stated from both; School of Airforce - Bodo in Norway and University of Bath, United Kingdom. Now that the evidences are open book, the monies Norway is holding back from her must be paid to her to facilitate her son's decent burial recognition!

Death is a phenomenon in society. Whereby no social class shall take advantage of the poor to hide forensic research from the next of kin.

Questions that are going to remain endless to Norwegian high circle in international politics are such as

- 996234843-AVwDHA.Org is a local Norwegian civic society organization, Norwegian authorities in this regard working hard to make this organization invisible? By torturing mother and son to the core. Just like Prof. Lumumba Otieno also say – Africa is tortured for no other reason but as above.
- What is the offence if Africa Diaspora in living in Norway strive for Africa Studies in Africa Spoken Languages reunion with Mother Language in Antiquity?
- If Norway high circles in international politics what to deny a hand in the killing of Kulwenzza-Otim, why has the recoding of the Oslo; January 2018 Racist Debate been removed on hearing a participant who challenged this debate. Her son has been murdered. The guilty are conscious?

7).

Every education person knows what is called a Library, Art Gallery, Museum etc. Nonetheless, such buildings are meaningless to Neo African if Africa Spoken Languages remain ignorant of the Mother Language in Antiquity. Library remain meaningless to Africa people themselves until that time when Africa spoken languages are studied in union with mother language in Antiquity in School Core-Curriculum Books. imagine colonial languages to Africa are Teachable from Pre-Primary School to the Highest Level. Why can't the HLPF see how unfair that must be! It is been 43 years following Diop and Obenga of this question to UNESCO Cairo Conference, what is your excuse? From where we stand to the close of SDG4 2030 what is the excuse for Africa Spoken Languages reunion with Mother Language in Antiquity and part of Core-curriculum?

Suggested Way Forward – the Aim with Mother Language – Our Common Good is advocating for implementation of SDG-4 quality education must concern Africa spoken languages reunion with Mother Language resources in Antiquity, and a part the School core-curriculum Goal.

Chapter 1. effort was made to introduce the challenge faced by modern Africa concerning contribution to the SDGs. Concerning implementation of SDG4 quality education must concern Africa School Curriculum reform. Africa must be mindful of writing down Africa Spoken Languages union with Mother Language in Antiquity. To foster quality job creation in Africa.

In the context, much effort was made to affirm Africa graduate Sankofa, go back to the source; Africa Origin of Civilization in Antiquity to get the skills right to develop a Resilient Africa graduate. That is how Foreign aid will work in the best interest of Africa if Africa Graduates Choose to Strive for knowledge of Self-identity, Spirituality, Custom etc. opposed to do development aid projects coercing Africa to do follow the money Projects.

Rebirth of knowledge

- Rebirth of knowledge is a custom.
- Renaissance is a custom.
- What a True Judge in the courtroom does is Custom.

Africa Sankofa go back to the source to get the Skills Right – is a rebirth of knowledge, a custom.

The case studies (see also the biographies here below), reveal that the best tool to abolish invented traditions embedded with racism and corruption is for global south to actively research in global north and put this research in school core-curriculum. This will create the Moral – if the Western want to research in global south, then equally global south must research in global north – this phrase is nothing different from the United Nations; HLPF/ EASG - June 2012 resolutions "future we want" and DSD opening for everyone to participate, come up with Added Value to become a Stakeholder in DSD.

Consequently, it is 996234843-AVwDHA.Org suggestion for "future we want"; 2022 he or she who want to enter to live, work and research in Africa must have at least a certificate in A Beginners Introduction to Africa Classic Studies. "A Beginners Introduction to Seshew Medew Netcher – Royal Scribes of Divine Words; there are a number of course centers, to choose from. 996234843-AVwDHA.Org corroborates with Sebauniversity.com On-line Studies, a full course study is 12 weeks; one day in a week; 2 hours session. But if one is a quick learner and good at self-studies, then it is possible to get ready for the final examination in a shorter time at a fee of $ 130 plus shipping fee. Of course, there are several beginners sSw mdw nTr centers. How different centers arrange the courses can also differ.

But where it is found written; "Netcher or nTr – Royal Scribes of Divine Words"? This must not be mistaken for the Christian Catholicism dating back to 2000 years of the Bible existence. You must think beyond that. Because You must think 10 000 – 17 000 BCA when Nile Valley science and technology man gave birth to knowledge. it was in Africa in Antiquity studying (not guessing) the Sounds in nature/ "nTr" that is how speech began in Antiquity. You may wish to learn how speech as we use speech in everyday life came to be. It all began from early man's association of ideas, see comparative method; Mboli 2010. Ranykemet language and Seshew mdw nTr – Royal Scribes of Divine Words date back to the old Kingdom ca. 5 000

8).
The Chants

Chant of courageousness both in hard times and progress –

Onyonyi oMutono; oNzelemba Saga – when communal wisdom blend in the meaning of hardworking

1. The majority;   Onyonyo omutono.
   Participants;   Nzeremba, onyonyi, onyonyo omutono nzeremba.
   The majority: Onyonyo omutono.
   Participants;   Nzeremba, onyonyi, onyonyo omutono nzeremba.

2. The minority;   Onyonyi oyoooooooo.
   Participants;   Nzeremba, aaaaaaaaa, Nzeremba
   The Minority;   Onkodoleeeeeeeeeeeee.
   Participants;   Nzeremba, aaaaaaaaa, Nzeremba.

3. The minority;   Onyonyo omutono.
   Participants;   Nzeremba, onyonyi, onyonyo omutono nzeremba.
   The minority: Onyonyo omutono.
   Participants;   Nzeremba, onyonyi, onyonyo omutono nzeremba.

4. The majority;   Ke kyussa kyussaaaaaaaaaaaaaaaaaaaa …
   Participants;   Nzeremba, onyonyi, onyonyo omutono nzeremba.
   The majority;   Ka sonya banna be.
   Participants;   Nzeremba, aaaaaaaaa, Nzeremba.

5. The majority;   Ohhh, banange e kyenkoba.
   Participants;   Hmmmmm.
   The majority;   Twabe tu kalete.
   Participants;   Hmmmmm.
   The Majority;   kaisi tukadunde.
   Participants;   Hmmmmm.
   The Majority;   Kaisi tukarile.
   Participants;   Hmmmmm.
   The Majority;   Oku bwitta okuwoma.

6. The minority;   Oh Nzeremba, nzeremba aaaaaaaaa, Nzeremba.
   Participants;   Oh Nzeremba, nzeremba aaaaaaa, nzeremba

   The minority;   Onkodoleeee, nzeremba aaaaaaa, nzeremba

   Participants;   Onyonyi oyoooh, nzeremba aaaaaa nzeremba

7. The minority;   Onyonyo omutono.
   Participants;   Nzeremba, onyonyi, onyonyo omutono nzeremba.
   The minority;   Onyonyo omutono.
   Participants;   Nzeremba, onyonyi, onyonyo omutono nzeremba.

8. The majority;   Onyonyo omutono.
   Participants;   Nzeremba, onyonyi, onyonyo omutono nzeremba.
   The majority;   Onyonyo omutono.
   Participants;   Nzeremba, onyonyi, onyonyo omutono nzeremba.

9. The majority;   Oooooo banange ekindi te.
   Participants;   Hmmmm.
   The majority;   Kawoma kokye.
   Participants;   Hmmmm.
   The majority;   Kaisi otumunyu
   Participants;   Hmmmm.
   The majority;   Okubwitta okuwoma
   Participants;   Hmmmm.

10. The minority;   Oo'nzerembaa,
   Participants;   nzerembaa aaaaaa nzeremba.
   The minority;   Onyoyi ooyoooh,
   Participants;   Nzerembaa aaaaaaa nzeremba

11. The majority;   Onyonyo omutono.
   Participants;   Nzeremba, onyonyi, onyonyo omutono nzeremba.
   The minority: Onyonyo omutono.
   Participants;   Nzeremba, onyonyi, onyonyo omutono nzeremba.

12. The majority;   Onanyere eika,
   Participants;   Yelilre eeeee yelire
   The majority;   Onanyere eika,
   Participants;   Yelilre eeeee yelire

13. The minority;   Onyonyi oyooooooo.
   Participants;   Nzeremba, aaaaaaaaa, Nzeremba
   The minority;   Onkodoleeeeeeeeeeee.
   participants;   Nzeremba, aaaaaaaaa, Nzeremba.
   The minority;   Ooo...nyonyi ... oyooooooo.
   All;   Nzerembaaaaaa haaaaa. Nzerembaaaaaaaaaah.

Chants on Mother Knee.

Acholi Saga of courageousness both in hard times and forwardness –

Tum bene is Acholi saga way to go Saga – when communal wisdom blend in the meaning of hardworking

Lead;	Tum, tum bene
Chorus;	Tum bene
Lead;	Tum, tum bene
Chorus;	Tum bene
…	…

Chaga People on the Foot of Mt Kilimanjaro Saga –

Host;   Simboli Nasikya?

Guest;   Safeyo, Simboli

Host;   Karibu Mugeni Tayari Chaga Mushroom Coffee

Guest;   Asante Mpenzzi wa Rohoo

Busoga people Saga –

Ga inssebikka gagya kwisubbi kusaaliza Nte …

Invoking the Soul of the Revered One

Kulwenzza-Otim;

To Call his name is to invoke his Soul and he responds –

> I have simply stepped into the next Life
>
> Whatever we are to each other, that we are still
>
> If you Call my name, you invoke the Soul/ Spirit
>
> Of me to speak to me in the easy way you always do
>
> Put no difference into your tone
>
> Wear no forced air of solemnity or sorrow
>
> Laugh as we always do together
>
> Play, smile, think of me, do a recitation of me
>
> Let my name be ever the household word as always
>
> Let it be spoken without effort
>
> Without heist or force in it
>
> Life means all that it ever it meant
>
> It is the same as ever it was
>
> There is absolute unbroken continuity
>
> Human Spirit Form is transformed to Ancestral Spirit Form

/Shm.m. Htp/

References

- Africa origin of Civilization – Myth or Reality; Cheikh Anta Diop 1973
- The intimacy of Spirit; Sobonfu Some 1997
- How language came to man in Africa – linguistic Comparative Method; Jean Claude Mboli 2010
- Paekche's Principle – the Great Secret of Asia by Bayemy Biyick 2014
- A beginner's introduction to sSw mdw nTr; Royal Scribes in Kemet Hieroglyphs transliteration and translation; Wudjau Iry Maat; 2015
- Research and Education; Will Curtis, Mark Murphy and Sam Shields 2014

  Jan 2018 Racism debate by Johan Galtung Q and A
  The video removed, by the debate management.

-
- http://psi424.cankaya.edu.tr/uploads/files/Hobsbawm_and_Ranger_eds_The_Invention_of_Tradition.pdf

- http://www.vukadarkie.com/cheikh-anta-diop-1974-unesco-symposium-in-cairo/

- https://sustainabledevelopment.un.org/index.php?menu=1298

- https://www.youtube.com/watch?v=wrohW9lhhI8

Biographies

- https://www.youtube.com/watch?v=Q5Gk36pUu1k

  28th Nov 2017 Uppsala University Lecture on Africa Poverty
- https://www.youtube.com/watch?v=vCm0JlGapP4

  Africa What to Demand 2018; conversation with sn. Mulocho Eric and snr.t wr.t Biibbi
- https://www.youtube.com/watch?v=x-dKbi-qOLg

  How Africa Culture History Matters
- https://www.youtube.com/watch?v=LcEDSmm56mc

  Jan 2018 Racism debate by Johan Galtung Q and A
  The video removed!

- https://www.youtube.com/watch?v=UiqUtVRd6DY
  The Great Nile Valley on Global Cardinal Orientation; by Wudjau Iry Maat 2017

- https://www.youtube.com/watch?v=VUZ_-bUrTNs
  NUPI; Oslo Norway; Foreign Affairs Debate 15th March 2018

- https://kunde.180.no/kp/default.asp?cmd=bilder&9hb9ek2c8wmdia408d8s

About the Author

Tolofaina KudambangaMwanna[7] is born and raised in Uganda. Back home she grew up in rural community looking to local community bridge builders; Men and Womyn who worked hand in hand opposed to the alleged Africa Womyn work more than men? The Africa Culture she grew is Africa Womyn is the centre in the community and the men are the protector! Womyn, children and the elderly should be protected in homes build by men. Womyn need not be obliged to work outside unprotected, fighting world life, falling huge trees for timber to haul into drum making! Through marital status she moved to Norway – Oslo 1990. Norway made the first impression to KudambangaMwanna with a Norwegian quote; "*det viktigst er å deltar ikke nødvedigvis seiren*" literally meaning "make a participation count more than being a winner". That quote adds-up to KudambangaMwanna's inspiration to keep herself informed. In Norway she created time to inform herself, taking on self-studies. 2016 she introduced the idea small groups in Africa and Norway to do On-line Studies in Mother language our common good, offered at Sebaunivercity.com. but when frightful information(s) shot in the air about; Kulwenzza-Otim's life taken 13th. May 2018, she told herself, "what had the mother of Patrice Desiree Lumumba done to the mechanism Corruption/ Racism Embedded in Invented Traditions? Answer; she gave birth to Africa Youth who Carry Our Promise for Tomorrow! What had the mother of Thomas Sankara done to the mechanism Corruption/ Racism Embedded in Invented Traditions? Answer; she gave birth to Africa Youth who Carry Our Promise for Tomorrow! Have your say.

---

[7] 2nd. June 2018 transposition of Comfort Onyee to KudambangaMwanna zenna e'izzo natuma KudambangaMwanna